Peak Strategies
Training Coaching Development

Pet Peeves & Problem People:
The Most Common Pet Peeves & Problem-People Problems

(and How to Handle Them)

Gwynne N. Dawdy, Ph.D.

Wasteland Press
Shelbyville, KY USA
www.wastelandpress.net

The Most Common Pet Peeves &
Problem-People Problems
(and How to Handle Them)
by Gwynne N. Dawdy, Ph.D.

Copyright © 2007 Gwynne N. Dawdy
ALL RIGHTS RESERVED

First Printing – April 2007
ISBN13: 978-1-60047-091-2
ISBN10: 1-60047-091-2

ALL RIGHTS RESERVED NO PART OF THIS
BOOK MAY BE REPRODUCED IN ANY FORM,
BY PHOTOCOPYING OR BY ANY ELECTRONIC
OR MECHANICAL MEANS, INCLUDING
INFORMATION STORAGE OR RETRIEVAL
SYSTEMS, WITHOUT PERMISSION IN WRITING
FROM THE COPYRIGHT OWNER/AUTHOR.

Printed In U.S.A.

To my mother, "the engineer", for inspiring this book and helping with its development.

This is for all of you who have to deal with problem people and pet peeves. Thank you for your input and good luck!

Contents

Prelude   9

Chapter One
Blaming and Complaining   17

Chapter Two
Feedback Fallout   35

Chapter Three
Attitudinal Outrage   47

Chapter Four
Lagging Leadership   71

Chapter Five
(De-) Motivational Mind-games   93

Chapter Six
Communication Corruption   *105*

Chapter Seven
Poor Presentation   *119*

Conclusion   *133*

About Dr. Dawdy   *135*

Index   *139*

Pet Peeves & Problem People:
The Most Common Pet Peeves & Problem-People Problems

(and How to Handle Them)

Prelude

After closely working with project managers, program managers, and other professionals, I came to the conclusion we all have to deal with problem people and pet peeve problems. Out of curiosity, I surveyed people to discover their people problems and pet peeves. Interestingly enough, many of the reported issues are universal and they transcend beyond profession, demographics, or organization. After discussing my workshops and this survey in detail, one engineer had noted, "Dr. Dawdy, you should design a workshop and write a book about these issues!" I laughed and tabled the idea.

The thought of a pet peeves and problem-people book continued to stir, until I could no longer ignore the opportunity. I further surveyed project managers from my workshops and decided to put these issues into writing. Thus, the Pet Peeves & Problem People book is born.

The issues I have received from my nation-wide survey are people-oriented. This was an intriguing find. These pet peeves also directly correlate with people problems. Let's face it; we all work with problem people. Some may go so far as to call these folks jerks (or other such terms). No matter what the description, we have to work with these individuals. Or do we?

Research has continually shown that poor attitudes, lack of respect, mistrust, and minimal motivation cost organizations a considerable amount of time and money. Many of your comments also note that a considerable amount of project time or money was lost because of the actions of problem people.

Can we "fix" these problems? I would love to answer with a definitive "yes" to this question. Unfortunately, it is not that easy. There is no magic wand or point-of-view gun that we can use to make the world right. We can not control the actions or behavior of others. What we can control our own actions, reactions, behavior, and communication. This may lead to prevention of or management of the pet peeves or people-problems.

In order to effectively manage these issues, we must first understand the behavior and the possible reasons for that behavior. This book will discuss the most common issues (and the possible reasons for those issues), and how to best manage those problems.

When managing these issues, we actually have to act. Thinking about how to change the situation does not change the situation, just like thinking about exercising is not the same as exercising. If a failure to act is part of the problem, then it may be that the pet peeve or problem-person may not be as bad as we perceive them to be. When only one person takes action, he or she may be considered a nag, even though the entire department is grateful for his or her actions. If this is the case, take a long hard look at your reasons for inaction, and thank the individual who takes risk and takes action. With action, you may see opportunity for advancement and for a high performance team.

It seems that working jerks are everywhere. Where they travel, they leave mental, physical or emotional turmoil and chaos. These jerks may be bosses, colleagues, or subordinates. They seem to make their appearance known in every aspect of the job. If you poll most people in the workplace, it is evident that one or more people within the organization are seen as problem people. What is sad is that these problem people do not seem to care about the problems they create with others. They either have their head in the sand, or they are very obstinate about their actions, decisions, and behaviors (with little regard to budget, time, or team members).

At some point, we hope these actions are met with consequences. Unfortunately, this may not occur within our preferred timeframe. In this, we must decide how to handle these pet peeves and problem people. With this decision, we also need to understand their behavior, their perspective, and their drives. It is my objective to assist in this matter through the writings in this book. Please also note that I do not have the background information to any of these issues, and since I am not an attorney, these suggestions are just that: suggestions based on behavioral methods. If you have a truly pressing issue with a problem person, it is important that you seek legal counsel and suggestion from multiple levels of your company before critical action is taken.

Pet Peeves & Problem People is written in a Q & A format, with your questions or pet peeves driving the text. It is divided into seven chapters. Each chapter represents various areas of the most common pet peeves and people problems reported to me.

Chapter One discusses the problems that involve blaming and complaining. I imagine it would be safe to wager that everyone has dealt with this issue, and those dealings were not necessarily pleasant. It is my intent to offer suggestions that may help to manage or prevent these issues from hurting your project.

Not only do we deal with the blame game, but we also have to manage people who do not handle feedback well. Either they do not know how to offer effective feedback, or they do not know how to accept the feedback given to them. Either way, we address issues dealing with these feedback fallouts in Chapter Two.

From ineffective feedback to complaints, and with everything in between, you will find the issues of attitudes. Attitudinal outrage discourages a team, derails a project and undermines the objectives. Many of us deal with attitudinal issues on a daily basis, and we can attest that this is tiresome and de-motivational. Chapter Three offers suggestions to manage or prevent attitudinal outrage in the workplace.

When we look at each of these issues, we also wonder, "What is going on with the leadership in this situation?" If we can't answer that question with confidence, then it may be that the leadership is lagging. When leadership is the issue at play, the game may turn ugly. Often, individuals in these situations ask, "should I stay or should I go?" While the answer may not be an easy one, Chapter Four will address some of the most common problems with lagging leaders.

Prelude

In connection with leadership, attitudes, feedback, and blame comes motivation. When people are not motivated to perform well, they may be motivated to perform poorly. This may lead to team dysfunction, project derailment, resource reallocation, or a combination thereof. While the topic of motivation is its own book (and I have written a book on motivation), it merits its own chapter here as well. Chapter Five discusses the de-motivational mind games that run amuck in many companies.

Throughout the surveys, I found these are not the only topics that tend to wreak havoc within the workplace. Another topic of importance to many of you was communication and the corruption therein. Since there were a number of communication pet peeves or people-problems, this topic certainly deserved addressing. Chapter Six focuses on communication corruption and offers strategies to manage these issues.

Last but not least is Chapter Seven, which voices your concerns on poor presentation. This includes many pet peeves regarding appearance, professionalism, respect and presentation. While we can't save the world from these atrocities, we can certainly change our behavior, responses, and methods of handling these problems.

If communication and assertive intervention are difficult for you, then these issues will continue. No one changes overnight, including people who are learning the skills of communication and assertiveness. It does take effort to induce change and to break the pattern of poor performance. It's up to you to weigh the benefits of action against the results of inaction.

Each of these issues was presented to me by leaders, project managers, engineers, city employees and other professionals across the United States. This book includes these issues in a forum that is meant to be informative and enjoyable. It also includes strategies to deal with these pet peeves and problem people from a behavioral perspective. As I've mentioned, there is no magic pill to fix these issues, but perhaps these strategies will lead to ideas you can use.

Chapter One:

Blaming and Complaining

My dearest friend is a high school counselor. She talks about her position as department chair and of the responsibilities involved for the measly $300 stipend. One of the unwritten "perks" of being the counseling department chair is that other staff members see her for guidance, for support, or to vent. There is tremendous turmoil and unsettlement in this high school, and staff members feel the need to vent to someone. Naturally, this someone is my friend.

I am sure this is not an isolated incident. From your responses, it sounds as if there are several companies in which morale is low and complaints are high. In these particular situations, it is apparent that more than one person causes this unsettlement. This chapter explores the constant complaining, blaming, or playing the victim of individuals in the workplace. We are not going to address the multiple possibilities that destroy the morale of an entire organization, although my friend and others in similar situations would love to address this issue. This complex topic of organizational complaining, blaming, and playing the victim would be a fantastic subject for another book.

Fault Finder

I have an employee who is constantly finding fault in others. He does not make his needs (resources, time, and personnel) known, yet when he has missed a milestone he blames others for not knowing his needs in the first place. When he misses these deadlines or is not capable of completing the task effectively, he blames others, even when we all know that the people he's blaming have nothing to do with his project.

It sounds like this person is made of rubber. Whatever you say bounces off him and sticks to you, just like the childhood rhyme. Unless someone defines the roles and addresses this issue directly, he may never get the message.

People can be conditioned. We push the envelope to see how far we can take things, and to discover the accepted boundaries. If boundaries are not set, the behavior continues. If you have not reviewed the expectations and role responsibilities with this individual, I may suggest this step. Another strategy is to ask the individual for his perception. Perhaps he is not aware that you or others on your team do not know exactly what it is that he needs. It may be that he is more introverted than extroverted and has trouble communicating his needs or concerns. In this, use coaching techniques to provide feedback and to set the boundaries and expectations.

If all of these things have been attempted, you may be sitting on a ticking time bomb. Some people are so unhappy with things that they will seek ways to destroy a team or derail a project. They may play the blame game in order to recruit additional members to their pity party, and to expand the feeling of discontent. A lack of motivation can devastate a team, especially if an individual is frustrated and aggressive. In this case, it may prove beneficial to simply ask this person, "What is it that you want?" His answer could be eye-opening.

On the one hand, if you review your steps to manage this problem, you may find that he can be coached to greater performance. On the other hand, you may find that you have done just about everything in your power to assist this person and nothing works. In this case, a visit with HR may be in order.

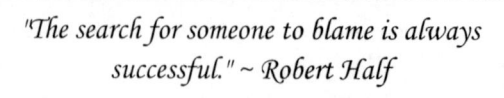

> "The search for someone to blame is always successful." ~ Robert Half

I Wasn't Told

I have a colleague who constantly blames her supervisor for not telling her things. I joked with her one day that her favorite saying was, "I wasn't told." I was hoping this subtle remark would prevent some future blaming, but it has not subsided and her motto continues to be, "I was not told." I know for fact that she was repeatedly told about these issues.

From the sound of things, your colleague suffers from selective listening. Placing blame on others for errors made is a defense mechanism. In this, many have an external locus of control, which means she blames others for her failures and successes.

It may be that your colleague needs additional reminders after the meeting. What I recommend for these situations is to draw out a charter signed by both parties, even if this is a simple summary-of-meeting minutes. When people activate multiple senses (in this case, auditory: communicating in the meeting, visual:

reading the minutes or summary of the meeting, and kinesthetic: signing of the charter or summary), they tend to recall the specifics of the meeting in a more accurate manner.

It could be that the choice of communication delivery does not agree with your colleague's preferred style. For instance, many people rarely read through the specifics of email. Thus, if you sent an urgent email to these folks with hopes that they would receive, read, and agree to the information, you may be disappointed. Some people prefer voicemail or face to face meetings. I would ask her what method of communication delivery she prefers, and follow that with the signed (electronic or by hand) agreement.

Not knowing the background to this issue, I also wonder if the message is difficult for your colleague to grasp. This could either be due to her job knowledge or to her sensitivity to feedback. With either of these, coaching may be useful. Remember, part of helping others excel relies on understanding their perspective. With coaching or open-ended questions, you may find the underlying issue and address it. It appears that whatever the background, you may need to see things as your colleague does in order to help her enhance her performance and change her motto.

Rumors

I oversee twelve engineers in an OEM project. One of these people tends to blame others rather than seek out the answers. She prefers to listen to rumors about other team members rather than discuss the issues with those individuals to find the truth. When it hits the fan, she ends up blaming everyone else for not knowing the truth.

I have found that this type of problem generally relates to a person's comfort level with conflict. Two things can be at play here. Either this person does not enjoy conflict and therefore finds it difficult to talk about an issue that may lead to conflict, or this person craves conflict and engages in this behavior to stir things up.

Either way, the behavior seems to be destructive to your team and to your project. It seems appropriate to have a discussion with her and discover her agenda. It is important to begin the conversation in a manner that is not over-bearing or threatening. Remember, you want to understand why she acts this way in order to best approach the situation. If she is uncomfortable with conflict and if the conversation you have with her is construed as over-bearing, she may shut down and you may not find the most appropriate solution to the problem.

In this conversation, it is important to point out your team's value on honesty, trust, respect, and truth. If she is new to the team, she may not recognize that her opinion will be met with open ears and minds, and this may prevent her from honestly speaking out.

Through your assertive listening and open-ended questions, you may discover which of the two issues are at play. If she is uncomfortable with conflict, then you can coach her through this by emphasizing respect and honesty. If you offer the open-door policy, emphasize this with her so she knows it is available

If she purposefully seeks conflict because it offers the stimulation she desires, then it is important to brainstorm with her ways to stimulate her profession. This could include greater intellectual challenge or healthy competition. In this, it is also important to emphasize the problems caused by her behavior and to clearly reiterate that blaming others instead of seeking the truth is not acceptable with your team.

Whichever the case, it is up to her to change her behavior and to seek out the truth. Perhaps this will shut down the rumor mill and open up the gates to greater productivity.

> "Our task now is not to fix the blame for the past, but to fix the course for the future."
> ~ John F. Kennedy

Criticized

I am a new manager to this group and I have found that a few individuals constantly complain or criticize my decisions. When it comes to project follow-through, they often rebel or question the actions of others. Not only that, but these few folks "tattle" when their colleagues error or when something is not done to specification.

This behavior seems to be taking the ship of fools to their final destination! I don't know if these actions were occurring prior to your arrival or not, but it is important to set your boundaries early and prevent this destructive behavior.

Being the boss, it may be very useful to pull each of these individuals into your office and address these actions. By asking questions and paraphrasing their responses, you may be able to discover the underlying reason for this disrespect.

Some reasons for this behavior could include a lack of motivation or a sign of job skill struggle. If it relates to motivation, ask what it is that motivates this person. With this personal list, you may be able to come up with some motivating solutions.

If the reason relates to job skill, training may be the answer. Perhaps this person has a fear of failure and that is why he tattles when others fault. Perhaps it is a fear of success that drives these behaviors. In this case, she may rebel because your project is on a path to success and this success could take her out of her element.

Often, saboteurs act to derail a project because they don't want the team to end (they are actually in a role they enjoy!). They also may shun success because it may lead to promotion or re-assignment. Perhaps they fear success because they don't agree with the project and don't want it to succeed. They look forward to being able to sneer, "I told you so."

Additionally, people who rebel and defy authority may do so because they think they can do better as leader, so they want the current leader to fail. If these individuals ache for leadership, when possible, give them a leadership role that feeds this drive.

The best way to handle these types of situations is through effective communication. This means using open-ended questions, active listening, and coaching skills. By discovering the reason behind the behavior, you may be able to curb the undesired behavior while improving morale and productivity.

> *"When any fit of gloominess or perversion of mind lays hold upon you, make it a rule not to publish it by complaints."* ~ Samuel Johnson

Complainers

I am surrounded by co-workers, supervisors, partners and vendors who complain. Whether their complaints are of the same topic or of different topics on the same day, I seem to be the magnet for complainers. How can I gently persuade others that I am no longer the sounding board for complaints?

First, you seem to be gifted at listening, and this may be why people flock to you when issues arise and complaints are high. This skill is a good thing, although it may not always seem so. Second, through your ability to active listen and attend to others, you may be able to gently quiet the complaints.
One of the initial steps is to take a proverbial stride back and objectively review the complaints heading your way. Are they of the same topic? Are you involved? Do you have knowledge that is supposed to help

with these issues? If the answer to these questions is a resounding "no", then you are truly a great sounding board that people seem to trust. In this, you can also address complaints without ruffling any feathers.

If the answer to these questions is "yes", then perhaps you are involved with the problem or are perceived as a necessary step in the solution. Objectively review the issue to understand why you are a magnet. With this, you may also understand how you can resolve the issue.

Regarding the first possibility, if you are not involved in these issues and are sought for your people-skills, then those skills can be used to steer the complaints in a more useful direction. Being that you are not the answer to everyone's problems, you can easily work with these individuals to brainstorm solutions to their issues. In this, you can also remind them that you have a job to do and that you will not be available to work with these issues all of the time. This emphasizes your importance to the project, and also forces individuals to personally take a step back and find solutions to their issues without automatically coming to you. This may also enhance communication between co-workers or between colleagues and supervisors.

Often, complainers seek a third party in order to simply vent or to gain followers of their misery. When people are acutely informed of these reasons, they may be able to better address the issues.

Whatever the reason or solution necessary, communication is key. If you ignore this issue, or continue to listen to these complaints behavior, you actually encourage this behavior

Too Much Work

One of my greatest pet peeves is when people complain about the tremendous amount of work they have, yet they seem to spend their time complaining instead of doing the work. It can lead to missed milestones and disgruntled team members. How can I handle this?

This type of complaint may be due to procrastination, which is usually a sign of frustration. With either of these possibilities, a sense of discomfort is present and could be the underlying reason for the behavior.

Procrastination seems to be a hot topic in organizations today. I have a free 1 hour teleconference regarding the topic (http://peakstrategies.net/goals.htm), and it seems to be well received by those interested in the issue of procrastination.

So, why do people complain instead their work? Perhaps they are frustrated because the specifics of the task were not outlined enough for their particular behavioral preference. Perhaps they are frustrated because they are not confident in the abilities required to complete the task. Perhaps the task at hand is not a task they enjoy.

When a task is not enjoyable, or when we are not confident in our abilities, we tend to toss it aside for something we enjoy. Most of the time, we may sit at the desk, answer phone calls, stare at the problem, and then get coffee. Along the way, we complain about the task and how much we have to do to complete it. This behavior actually rewards procrastination!

In order to curb complaints or procrastination, people need to set clear goals. For instance, commit to working on the task in question for at least 45 minutes before you get coffee. A brief coffee break is the reward, so reward yourself for accomplishing the task, not for procrastinating and complaining. When we set goals that include opportunity for procrastination and complaints, there must be a reward after the goal is achieved. This can be simple or complex, personal or professional, acknowledgement or monetary.

Individuals who fall into the pattern of procrastinate-complain-reward may need to be coached to a productive pattern of behavior. If they truly want to do their part and simply do not like the task at hand, establish a system of goals and rewards. If these individuals do not have a strong understanding of what is expected, they may need greater detail and role definition. Whatever the case, both parties should address this behavior and establish a clear set of guidelines regarding procrastination and project deadlines. Keep in mind, the longer you procrastinate in addressing this issue, the worse it gets.

> *"He cannot complain of a hard sentence, who is made master of his own fate."* ~ Johann Friedrich Von Schiller

He Doesn't Work

One of my colleagues complains because one of her colleagues does not do his work. She does not address this issue with him, but complains to everyone else. Why does she do this and how can I stop it?

The fact that you are willing to help your colleague with this issue is commendable. In order to best address this, there are a couple of variables we need to consider.

One of the greater variables is her comfort level with assertive communication. She may engage in the communication style that shies from conflict. If she tends to sway from conflict and unpopular decisions, it may be easier for her to sweep the issue under the rug and hope it goes away. When it does not, she may become more frustrated and this is when she complains the most. If this is the case, it is important for you to let her know that her actions are not helping the team. If a passive behavior was chosen when assertive actions were necessary, the undesirable behavior (your colleague's co-worker's lack of productivity) was actually encouraged instead of discouraged. People do not have to be mean or ruthless to address these issues, but people do need to be assertive. In this, attend to the reason why this person is unproductive and address the job skills or motivational factors that may be in play.

When you work with your colleague, you also need to be assertive and solution-focused. Ask her what strategies she has used to deal with her co-worker. Discover what her role is in this situation. Perhaps she is a part of the problem or perhaps she is just a sounding board for her co-worker. If she understands why her co-worker confides in her (even if he just complains), then she may be able to help her co-worker excel.

Playing the Victim

My team member constantly complains, as if she is a victim of the company or of the leaders in the department. She doesn't do anything about the issues in her complaints. My company calls this, "learned helplessness" and it is very difficult to break people of this mindset.

I see how this would be a great pet peeve. In this situation, it appears she may have a bad attitude, a lack of desire to excel, and the need to be in the midst of conflict and drama.

In order to address this situation, one needs to ask her what she would do to remedy the situation if she had the magic "cure all" wand. Her answer may be outrageous, but if you continue to fine tune the options to something she can control, she may feel in control.

People also complain and play the victim to simply attract attention. The more attention they attract, the more often they play the victim. This behavior (complaining) receives a reward (attention) and thus the pattern continues. In order to decrease the undesirable behavior, you have to decrease the rewards. In order to increase a desirable behavior, you have to increase the rewards. Rewards do not have to be monetary or materialistic. Rewards can simply be attention, pleasure, joy, belonging, or any other number of reinforcements.

Your company is accurate in that this can be a case of learned helplessness. As the term implies, this behavior is learned, which also means it can be unlearned. In order to unlearn a behavior such as this, it is critical that the undesired behavior is not rewarded in any way. When she acts in a desirable manner, she is attended to or rewarded. This way, she learns a new way to behave that is more productive and effective than playing the victim.

This behavior change does not happen overnight, but it does happen.

"Some people change when they see the light, others when they feel the heat." ~ Caroline Schroeder

Chapter Two:
Feedback Fallout

Feedback is a critical component of improvement. Without a scoreboard, players don't have a strong sense of how they are doing or who is winning. Without grades, students may not grasp how well they are doing in a course. Without feedback, people may not be confident in their skills in the workplace.

In fact, I knew of a woman whose story is the perfect example of the importance of feedback. It is such a fitting story, that I believe I also discuss this example in my Motivation and Inspiration book.

A young woman, we'll call her Karen, worked with a firm for many years. She was a hard worker, dedicated and driven. Her supervisor usually kept in contact with Karen and supplied her with feedback so

Feedback Fallout

she knew where she stood. This feedback helped her correct any errors included praise for her higher levels of performance.

A new team member was assigned to her team. We will call him Trevor. Karen's supervisor took extra time to work with Trevor, but this also meant he spent less time giving Karen feedback. Trevor's performance continued to increase with the coaching, mentoring and feedback he had received. But something had occurred with Karen...

Karen's supervisor was not concerned with Karen's performance, as she had always proved her ability and rose to the challenge presented to her. He was taken aback when he noticed her performance slip in the same time frame he worked with Trevor. At first, he made this issue more complex than it was, as he assumed that Karen had sabotaged her own performance because Trevor had excelled. This was not the case.

When Karen's supervisor sat down with Karen, he discovered that Karen did not realize her performance slipped below her usual levels. When they reviewed the tasks and productivity, Karen saw where she could improve. They realized her performance slipped simply because she had not received the feedback she needed.

While this seems like a simple story, it is true and it happens all too often. A lack of feedback or poor feedback presentation can be the reason for shoddy performance, decreased productivity, and low morale. It may also be one of the most common reasons why people seek answers from others, whether in form of gossip, water-cooler conversation, or simple guessing. We all know where these methods of fact-finding can lead. More often than not, it leads to conflict and rumors. From this, we waste time trying to correct the miscommunication, which would have been prevented with clear and timely feedback.

News via Gossip

I admit -- it happens in my office. Because of a lack of communication from management of what is REALLY going on, the rumor mill, corridor gossip, and peer conversation remains the only way of receiving feedback.

It appears your office suffers from Feedback Fallout. It is an illness that plagues many companies. No matter what the reason, if it is not treated, the project and morale greatly suffer.

Contact your supervisor regarding the chain of communication and follow it accordingly. This is not to say that the corridor gossip is not necessary. Studies show this is a very important aspect of the entire communication picture. However, it is not the most effective method of communication regarding project issues, personnel inquiry, or change.

There seems to be a lack of feedback from all levels. Perhaps those with the answers don't realize there are looming questions or confusion. This is a lack of feedback from your group to theirs. Perhaps those with the answers don't realize they do not provide clear enough feedback. Either way, it is important for representatives of both parties to connect and outline the communication issues in play.

Tunnel-vision Boss

A past supervisor of mine would not give me a good performance review because there weren't any organizational goals in play and he could not think of any ways that I contributed to HIS success.

This is a supervisor who can't see the forest through the trees. Because he did not emphasize the positive contributions you have made to your project, your supervisor actually encouraged lower performance levels. This will certainly not enhance his success, much less yours.

A performance review should include an individual's performance, big and small, good and bad. What an amazing concept. It speaks volumes that your supervisor neglected to support your successes, even if they weren't directly related to the organizational goals. To be honest, I do not see a cohesive team or a high performance department led by someone like your supervisor.

This is a good lesson for all. When providing feedback, it is important to include all aspects. Furthermore, positive feedback is just as critical as constructive feedback. Negative feedback can be detrimental to a project, so if the goal is to improve performance, be sure that the feedback is constructive, not negative or out of spite.

What is the difference? Negative feedback is typically offered in a way that makes a person feel bad, without offering any ideas or methods to improve. Constructive feedback is given in such a way that it points out the errors, and it offers (or encourages) strategies for improvement and success. Constructive criticism (feedback) empowers individuals, whereas negative feedback tears a person down without option or confidence.

It is important to address the concern with this review in the meeting or soon thereafter. If your supervisor is as egotistical as it seems, ask what he would need for you to do to earn a good review. If you earn a good review, he earns a good review. This makes him look good.

If your supervisor is completely inept in the ways of feedback, it may be time to seek other options.

> *"They may forget what you said, but they will never forget how you made them feel."* ~ Carl W. Buechner

Right on Track

I have an employee who was assigned as a lead to a portion of my project. When I visit with her on the phone or in her office, she seems unorganized. When I ask her for a status report, all she says is, "I am right on track."

My first question is, "Is this her usual m.o.?" If she usually appears unorganized and scattered but pulls off her part by deadline and with little error, she may be one of those free-spirited people who seems unorganized but works comfortably with her own awkward structure. If this is the case, and if you need a response that is more definite and more detailed than, "I am right on track," then you need to emphasize the importance of this status to her. Many people are quite unaware of the importance of these reports. They may simply think that people are "checking up on them."

If this person is truly unorganized and is falling behind without the wherewithal to ask for assistance, then it is time to jump in and coach through the obstacles. The best way to find out if this is the case is to request a lengthier, oral status meeting. This virtual or local meeting could occur over coffee, and should certainly occur in a room where she will feel more comfortable and not threatened. (Think of the principal's office... very little honest success was brainstormed while in this office and under a sense of fear).

In this meeting, re-emphasize her strengths and why she was assigned the lead to this piece of the project. Follow that with your need to have a more detailed status update of her project portions. Perhaps discuss difficulties others have had as project lead, and ask her what is difficult for her in this piece. Use solution-focused brainstorming techniques to move beyond these difficulties and to keep you in the loop.

In the end, feedback flows both ways. If she understands that it is just as much her responsibility as it is yours, you may experience greater levels of communication.

Later Never Comes

One of my greatest pet peeves is when I ask for more feedback for my project and the response I get is, "I will get the information to you later" and then later never comes.

This information must not be important to these people, or "later" would come sooner. If this is important to you, it is necessary to make it important to them. Tune in to their favorite radio station (WIIFM: we all know it--What's In It For Me) and emphasize why it is important to them to get this information to you.

The other possibility is that this information is important to them, but they are so swamped that the corridor conversation took a back seat to urgency. In this case, it is acceptable to phone with a kind reminder for this information. Again, explain to them why this is both urgent and important to you, and ask if there is anything you can do to expedite the distribution of information. If they understand that they are important to you, and that the information they provide is also important to you, they may be more conscientious about getting the information to you in a timely manner.

Foggy Feedback

I had a supervisor who did not offer clear expectations or feedback to employees. He also did not take the time to know what we (employees) did and how we did it. He not only did not understand our methods, he did not support us when vendors or partners questioned our techniques. Therefore, the feedback he gave was incomplete and we had little to go on.

It sounds like *he* has little to go on! If this supervisor is still in position, it isn't because of his leadership abilities. Let's turn this into a learning lesson for us all.

When newly appointed to a team, it is critical to take the time to meet and understand each team member and their preferences. If this forming phase is skipped, it may be nearly impossible to become a high performance team with great levels of productivity.

From here, a team may still sift through the storming phase of conflict and choices. If this is handled with grace, dignity and respect, the team can build great levels of trust and honesty. This is important to note, as a situation may call for that trust. For instance, when a vendor or partner questions the methods used or the deliverables in cue, a team with high levels of trust and respect will also have a leader who supports and defends their decisions. In this, the leader will understand the chosen methods and can explain this with great detail to the vendors. This may appease the other party while empowering the team to heightened levels of productivity.

Finally, when a supervisor understands each of these aspects, he can give a thorough and skilled report. This also includes providing feedback that not only helps to re-engage employees, but also helps to keep those employees engaged.

> *"We are what we repeatedly do. Excellence, then, is not an act, but a habit."* ~ Aristotle

ESP Expectations

My supervisor has one big flaw: She does not share information with us, but she expects a thorough understanding from us.

So, she doesn't tell you anything, but expects you to understand what it is that she did not tell you. It sounds simple enough.

When I discuss teams and team issues, much of it relates back to a lack of communication. One of the most common culprits is the "message known to sender, message unknown to receiver" error. In this, the person providing the information has a message he wants to send, and he thinks he is sending it, but the receiver does not hear it at all. In fact, the receiver may not even recognize that a message was sent!

This definitely should be addressed before it causes major damage to your project and your team. This means communication has to begin somewhere, and that somewhere should start with your supervisor.

You may even coach her. We can coach on many levels, and coaching for greater communication can be very powerful for the entire team. Ask her what she expects from the team in regards to communication. Find out what would make her happy as a supervisor in relation to the team. Explore options to enhance meetings or feedback. Discover whether she is more concerned with the project or the process, with the details or the big picture, with the team or the product. Then, use her concerns to emphasize the need for heightened and more explicit feedback.

If you connect with her on the issues with which she is concerned, she may be more apt to connect with you on the details that you need. I would guess that this supervisor does not intentionally withhold information, as most in leadership positions wish their team and project well. If this is a correct assumption, she may not be aware of the miscommunication until it is too late.

Feedback is very critical and someone who is not feedback savvy may have greater troubles.

To open the communication gates, one actually has to communicate. That step can begin with you and your team.

> *"The problem with communication... is the ILLUSION that it has been accomplished."* ~ George Bernard Shaw

Chapter Three:
Attitudinal Outrage

The way we perceive a situation may directly link to our attitude, and vice versa. When a team is flogged by bad attitude, the project may be sabotaged. Believe it or not, an attitude is something we can control.

One of the best ways to better an attitude is to embrace objectivity. This means stepping away from the situation and giving the people involved the benefit of the doubt. I committed to this while I travel, and it has done wonders.

For instance, prior to my decision to have a good attitude, in bad traffic, I may have snapped more quickly than I do now. My red-headed temper would kick in and everyone around me would be miserable thanks to my attitude. Nothing was accomplished.

Attitudinal Outrage

Now, when someone cuts me off in traffic or cuts in at airport security, I force a smile and give them the benefit of the doubt. Perhaps this person has an emergency, perhaps they suffer from a migraine, perhaps their car is falling apart and they need to exit... I use whatever excuses I can to keep a positive attitude.

My other thought is this: If I were right and this person had just experienced some traumatic event and I threw a tantrum because they were slightly rude, how badly would I feel knowing I added to their horrible day? Personally, I would feel awful knowing I chose to take the low road and react with a negative attitude.

Here is an example that I heard somewhere. I am not sure if it was in a book or in one of my workshops, but I do remember the story. One day, a woman was on her way home on the subway. She was tired from a long, trying day at the office. A father and his two young children sat near her on the train. His children were a bit rambunctious and were drawing the attention of other adults. The father did not seem to notice.

The woman had had enough. She looked at the man and snapped, "Can't you control your children?" The man looked up at her with a grim expression and slowly said, "I am sorry. We just came from their mother's funeral."

The woman was shocked and admitted that she felt a pit in the bottom of her stomach when she heard his response. It explained the behavior and the fog this gentleman seemed to be in. She apologized and began to think about her reactions.

This story reiterates the importance to give the other person the benefit of the doubt, especially when the response will not affect your status one way or the other. This is not to say that being pleasant means being a pushover. In fact, when people are pleasant, statistically, they have a greater chance of receiving the information or results they desire.

Attitudes carry a great distance. What type of attitude will you have?

"Then, without realizing it, you try to improve yourself at the start of each new day; of course, you achieve quite a lot in the course of time. Anyone can do this; it costs nothing and is certainly very helpful. Whoever doesn't know it must learn and find by experience that a quiet conscience makes one strong." ~ Anne Frank

Undermining Saboteur

I work with someone who has an undermining characteristic about him. He

Attitudinal Outrage

tries to assert his view onto the project team. When he disagrees with the approach that the team approved, he becomes very negative and acts like a project saboteur.

I think you've got this guy pegged. Because of personality traits or because of experience, some people are naturally more pessimistic in nature. While it does not sound as if this is an issue of optimism vs. pessimism, it does sound as if an attitude may be in cue to destroy the project.

In my Teaming for Excellence program, we discuss saboteurs. What encourages this behavior? This simple question may have complex answers. Initially, it may be that this person has either a fear of failure or a fear of success. Furthermore, a saboteur may be misplaced in task assignment and is simply miserable, seeking to recruit other people to join in the misery. Finally, this person may be angry because of job insecurity or because he was passed up for promotion or reassignment. Whatever the reason, he does not seem happy, nor does it appear that he wishes the project team well.

With this attitude, an assertive is in order. Coaching and solution-focused brainstorming may be the most effective types of discussion for this issue. In this, the person may explain why he is in such disagreement with the team, and why he is consciously or unconsciously undermining

Pet Peeves & Problem People

the project's success. Address as many issues as you can and brainstorm with him to find a collaborative and cooperative solution that is win-win for everyone.

If he is willing to change, the change may not happen overnight, but over time, you will likely see the desired behavior. If he is unwilling to change, then seek out the appropriate channels to correct this issue, even if it means his reassignment.

Remember, attitudes are a personal reaction to a situation. We can not change someone else's attitude, no matter how much we want to! They have to want to change, and they have to commit to change in order for that desired attitude to take shape. All we can do is point out the surface issue, try to discover the underlying problem, brainstorm realistic solutions, and establish an action plan for change. This includes revealing what actions may take place if the attitude does not change.

It Can't Be Done

Here is one pet peeve of mine: Negative non-thinkers. What is this, you ask? This is someone who consistently replies to a request to do something with, "It can't be done," or "I don't have time to do this." Then I have to sit with her and prod her to take on this task. After discussion occurs, she realizes this task won't take as much time or resources as she thought—or didn't think!

Negative non-thinkers are everywhere. The reason for their existence varies, but in all cases, it is necessary to weigh their motivation and job skill. If you discover that they hesitate to take on these tasks because they have low confidence, then they need to experience success, even if these successes are small. This means offering more positive feedback with jobs that they do and do well. It also means asking them what motivates within a task and then be sure to emphasize those aspects whenever feasible.

In this case, I see there is also a commitment issue. From first glance, it appears as if she hesitates to add any further tasks to her current job load, even if it is part of her project. Again, this could be because of a lack of confidence. It could also relate to her current workload (yes, some people are extremely overwhelmed and one more task may appear to break them).

Furthermore, this issue may exist because she does not agree with the task objective, or perhaps the task does not align with her personal values. When we are in conflict with the objective or the values within a project, we rarely perform at optimal levels.

The best way to discover the underlying reason is to take a moment to ask her why she hesitates when you know she can be successful. Whatever her reason, you can address it and support the success and her confidence throughout the task. This may also pave the road for greater commitment and project support in the future.

Emotional Apathy

In my organization, there are a few individuals who are apathetic. This can be a problem when others perceive this as a lack of concern regarding the impact of actions on the department or on the work team.

This seems to be an issue in many organizations. With the expectation of being professional comes the inability to express concern or satisfaction when needed. I also see this as a greater issue in areas where logical thinkers comfortably abide, leaving emotional context at the door. There is a time and a place for everything, including an appropriate expression of concern, satisfaction, or disappointment.

So, the question is: do they *appear* to be apathetic, or *are* they apathetic? When someone appears not to care, they may actually care a great deal but choose to not express this. When we take reactions at face value, we may offer a great disservice to the individuals involved. Remember, people are very complex, and through nature or nurture, we may act or react differently to situations.

It may be time to approach the key individuals and ask their opinion and their perception in regards to the issues within your department. You may discover that they are as disturbed as you are, but perhaps they do not think they can do anything about it, therefore, why invest the emotional energy?

You may discover they do not perceive these issues as you do, and thus never considered them to be of threat to the team's productivity. If this is the case, it would be beneficial to discuss your perceptions and concerns, as they may be able to see your point of view.

If these individuals are heavily focused on the results and the product, it may also be useful to include how these concerns negatively impact the team's progress and how they hamper results. From this, your team may collaborate on ideas that would suit all involved and would address the issues of perceived apathy.

As with most people-problems, the key is communication. If we simply complain about the other's perspective or reactions without fully understanding those responses, then we may make a situation much worse than it truly is.

> *"If you are distressed by anything external, the pain is not due to the thing itself, but to your estimate of it; and this you have the power to revoke at any moment."* ~ Marcus Aurelius

Curbed Creativity

I have worked with a woman who was so concerned about keeping her boss "happy" that she lost the value of risk-taking. She seemed to be walking on egg shells and rarely contributed new ideas or refreshing product possibilities.

With little background to this incident, it appears that she fears losing her job. When people have been continually laid-off because of organizational decision, they tend to lose a sense of control. In this, they also lose the security needed to take heightened risk within the project. If this is the case, perhaps this woman was never assured that the team expects and respects new ideas and valued risk-taking. In this, re-address those expectations.

This step would be similar to the forming stage of teamwork, in that you would address expectations, values, role definitions, and overall objectives. Emphasize the value of risk and creativity and include ideas to reinforce this behavior. Her boss should also be included in this conversation, to simply review the team's dynamics or to verify the team is on its way to becoming a high performance unit.

Another possibility for this behavior is her desire to advance or to be reassigned to a different project. If this is the case, she may attend to the future aspect instead of the current reality of risk and project creativity. If this new position is in the near future, she may be well on her way to another assignment and you will be introducing yourselves to a new team member. With this, you will still be reconnected to the forming stage where expectations and role definitions are discussed.

Whatever the case, you may communicate your expectations and your value on risk and creativity. Whether this is with this woman or a new team member remains to be seen.

Instant Promotion

Once I had a college hire who joined my team. After only a couple of months on the job, he expected to be promoted. I was caught off guard by the expectations of this new hire. After talking with other managers, I discovered this was not an isolated

Pet Peeves & Problem People

incident. *I guess you could say that the attitude of expecting instant promotion is a pet peeve of mine.*

I can see how this attitude would be a pet peeve. I think I would be taken back by the demand of promotion by a new hire. So, is this a collegiate expectation or is this a big dream by ambitious college grads?

Either way, this issue begs for a simple conversation outlining the typical chain of events for promotion or advancement. Keep in mind that this topic may not have been addressed with him, so this may be a simple informational meeting. If he is ambitious, try not to squelch those ambitions, but outline his goals in connection with team and organizational objectives. What are the usual milestones for promotion? Has this person met those milestones? Did he meet the team and organizational expectations necessary for advancement? By discussing these usual practices, your new hire may have better bearings regarding his promotional status.

This is not to say that some new hires may not set the world on fire within their first few months and deserve advancement. However, statistics reveal that this is unusual.

Bad Attitude Bob

My team included a gentleman who was going through a rocky, transitional personal period in his life. We sympathized with him. However, he began to bring his bad attitude into work because of his personal situation. At first, we were accepting and felt badly for him. Now, I can see that his negative attitude is hurting his performance and the performance of the team.

As I have mentioned, an attitude is one of the components needed for high performance. Additionally, we can change our own attitude. This gentleman has had a rough go of it for a while, but this does not give him the right to take it out on others. Unfortunately, he does not see the workplace as a space to escape from the personal woes. I am not sure if you can make him see it that way, but a conversation about this problem is due.

When I coach others who struggle with this issue, I relay an analogy relayed to me from a fantastic mentor (Dr. Michael Lillibridge of the PeopleMap system). I do remember the story because it hit home and I knew I could use it with clients.

Imagine four new barrels of paint. Each barrel has fresh paint of a different color: one red, one blue, one yellow and one green. Each barrel represents a different aspect of your life. For instance, the red represents your personal life, the blue represents your work life, the yellow represents your spiritual life, and the green represents your financial life.

Imagine that you have been home with your family all weekend. It has been a rocky weekend because you got into a car wreck and your children were taken to the hospital with minor injuries. This is your red paint. In this analogy, you are covered in red paint because you have been in the barrel of red all weekend.

Now, it is Monday morning and time for work. Your mood is sour because of the weekend experience. What happens if you jump from the barrel of red paint into the barrel of blue paint (representing work)? Will the barrel of blue paint stay a crisp, clean blue? What color does it change to? More than likely, it looks like a murky brown. You have mixed the colors. Then, if you jump from this barrel into the green barrel (representing your financial life), the green barrel may also become murky. The pattern continues.

This is not to say that we don't bring our personal problems to work or our professional problems home. It is nearly impossible to separate various aspects of our lives. However, deep breaths and self-talk into a more objective frame of mind do work. Consider this as a mental bath. Debrief what has just occurred and prepare

Attitudinal Outrage

to step back to an objective frame of mind for the next task. This mental bath may help decrease the number of times people bring bad attitudes to work, which destroys the barrel of blue paint. This also helps to decompress before returning home, so we don't kick the dog out of sheer frustration! So instead of jumping directly from one barrel to another, take a mental bath before jumping into the next barrel of your life. It works. Try it.

When you work with someone who suffers in some part of his life, it may be effective to encourage him to use the workplace as a safety zone or a bunker. If he can re-address his perspective, his attitude may shift to neutral, at least.

> *"Human beings, by changing the inner attitudes of their minds, can change the outer aspects of their lives." ~ William James*

Drama Queen

I have a kind young woman on my work team who starts each day with a 15 minute review of her personal life. When something "tragic" happens in her personal life, she is the epitome of the drama queen, *and this attitude affects her work and the work of others.*

Kindness comes in all shapes and sizes. If she were truly kind, she would be considerate of your time or productivity and keep some of these problems to herself.

Besides teaching her the value of the "mental bath", she may also benefit from learning the value of personal privacy. You mentioned that she is a kind person, and this can be favorable to you in your discussion with her. Again, her attitude may reflect the fact that she does not perceive her actions the same way that the rest of your team does. In this, emphasize the value of time. It may also be worth the moments to review the story, "The Boy Who Cried Wolf." While she may not be crying wolf, her crying over little things will decrease the value of the big things that are worth her tears and the ears of others.

Social Loafers

My greatest peeve as a supervisor is when people only do enough to get by, and in a group setting, they end up letting the rest of the team do most of the work.

In organizational psychology (and sociology), we call this "social loafing."

Attitudinal Outrage

Social loafing occurs when a team member does little or nothing to help the remainder of the team. I remember working with social loafers when I was in college and was assigned team projects. This experience was so frustrating. To know that this type of behavior continues in the workplace does not sit well with many of us, I am sure.

How do you handle social loafers? Keep in mind that most of the time a social loafer is not going to walk into your office and complain that he is loafing on the job. The complaints will come from everyone else on the team. Much of the time, this is preventable if you have a strong, well-defined forming phase, where each person's role, responsibilities, and job assignments are clearly laid out. In this, it is also important to make certain you have these expectations in writing within your team charter and that each member agrees to and signs the document. From this, you would give each individual a copy of the charter for their reminder and review.

If this has occurred, the next step would be to talk directly with the social loafer. Ask him what he sees as his role and responsibility before you review the agreed charter. In this, you try to see the issue from his perspective. If he agrees with the charter (and remembers his responsibilities), then there may be a latent reason for his slacking behavior. Perhaps he fears he will not be able to perform as well as other team members. Perhaps he is uncertain with the parameters of the task. To get him moving again, review the roles and responsibilities and address his concerns.

You also need to address the fact that this behavior is not acceptable and that future involvement is critical to his success and the project's progress.

> *"I like the word 'indolence.'*
> *It makes my laziness seem classy."*
> *~ Bern Williams*

Administrative (non-)Assistant

My administrative assistant was assigned to me. She spends all day on the phone with personal calls. When I need the support, she is not there to give it. Her mood sours when I ask her to do things, as she doesn't think she has to support me. My boss completes her review and this does not seem to help my dilemma.

If you have not already assertively addressed this situation, it bears addressing. If you recall, I noted that people can be conditioned. It sounds as if your administrative assistant has conditioned you to leave her to do what she pleases on company time. To correct this, the two of

Attitudinal Outrage

you (and perhaps three of you if you feel your boss needs to be included) should have a come-to-Jesus meeting. In this, you would address the job description, the hours spent on personal calls, the number of times she neglected your tasks and the lack of support that should be provided.

Not all of our meetings are going to be coaching or questioning type of meetings. There are times when an assertive approach and a factual foundation are necessary. This appears to be one of those times.

If her behavior and mood do not improve, document this and consider a visit with your boss. There may be a reason why she is being obstinate, and if there is more you should know, perhaps your boss has the answers.

If your boss seems oblivious and you feel this issue is a big problem, you may want to seek guidance from HR.

Preparing to Fail

For this survey of pet peeves, I was quickly able to come up with my biggest pet peeve. My greatest pet peeve is when people spend time preparing for failure in a project versus assuming success in a project. Why can't people give equal time to the preparation of both success and failure?

There could be a number of legitimate reasons for preparing for the failure of a project. Many team members often wonder how far the project will go if the only focus is failure.

I worked with a team who had experienced this multiple times. They were given a project, and then that project was cancelled after an intensive commitment of time and resource. They were given a second project, and this project was also cancelled. Both projects had a focus of failure over success. By the time this team was given the third project assignment, no one worked on the project until the first milestone was near. That is when they realized the project was truly going to happen, and they scrambled to complete the necessary tasks before the first deadline.

The attitude on this project was originally one of skepticism. This quickly changed to drive and dedication once the team knew the organization was supporting the project.

It seems that by planning for failure, organizations may limit their losses in case vendors or external parties pull the plug. I agree that this can be a self fulfilling prophecy. We tend to see what we focus on, and if we focus on failure, that is what we see. This focus and preparation may not be easy to change at the organizational level, but your department can shift attention.

Ask your team members about their greatest project successes. What made them successful? How can they transfer these experiences to your current project? If you use open-ended questions that focus attention on successes and not failure, you may discover many areas where your team can truly excel. You may also find ways to motivate your team and reward them for hitting their milestones.

Resentful

I had an interesting professional experience. A new position was created, and I was chosen to fill that position. One co-worker was so resentful of my appointment that she literally did not speak to me during my first week on the job! Her attitude softened as she adjusted to my position, but I know there are other people who have experienced this situation and the moods may have never recovered.

This may be the green giant rearing its ugly head, and by that I mean Envy. We have discussed how we can not change other people's reactions or attitudes, but we can change our own. In this, know that if we react more positively to a change, then that change may be met with adjustment and acceptance, as may have been the case here.

Of course, some colleagues may feel downright betrayed or passed over, and this does not help the change. If you feel your co-worker's attitude is hindering your performance, take her for coffee and discover the reason behind her animosity. If you do not get any information from this meeting, you could take the next step and visit with your supervisor. Perhaps mediation is necessary, even if it is more for her attitude than for yours. Even if we can't change her attitude, we can collaborate for a win-win situation, and that can motivate her to change her attitude and her reaction.

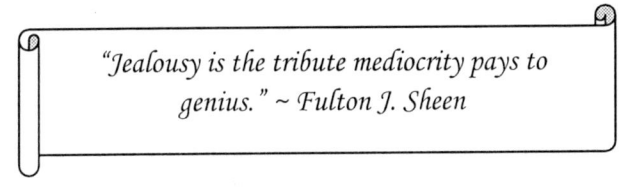

> *"Jealousy is the tribute mediocrity pays to genius." ~ Fulton J. Sheen*

It's All About Me

My boss seems like he has narcissistic traits. He thinks NO ONE is important but him, thus we are all inferior. You can imagine the attitude and morale in our office. Funny thing is, when he is away, we work well together and enjoy our team.

Attitudinal Outrage

This doesn't sound like a funny situation at all. Believe it or not, narcissism is an actual disorder, diagnosable using the current edition of the Diagnostics and Statistical Manual. It is truly difficult to work with an honest-to-goodness narcissist. Working with individuals who are simply full of themselves may be more feasible.

If his greatest drive is his drive to be the best, then you can use this in your favor. Emphasize how your team can work to improve in order for him to be number one. Ask what he seeks from his team and what he expects from you. Find out what he also expects of himself to encourage the team's top performance. If you focus the conversation on his drive (being the best) and slyly weave into the conversation your needs (being appreciated or respected), then perhaps your boss will see the light.

Usually, when these types of leaders do not see the light, they drown in their own darkness, as no one is there to offer support. It seems a fitting demise to their leadership title, since most of the time these supervisors did not support their team when the team needed it.

As far as your team's situation, it appears as if you have great cohesion and morale when the big cat is away. Let the mice play, and keep in mind you have power over your reactions and your attitudes.

Helping or Hindering

One fellow on my team is always so helpful-- even to a fault. He always helps others and does not concentrate on his own work. Sometimes, this puts us behind, as his work and timing are important to our work.

Many people do not work well with conflict. Because of this, they may find it difficult to say no. They have a tremendous knack to resolve conflict and to aid in personal issues. If these people are few and far between in the workplace, they are highly sought (even to a point where it is difficult for them to pass up these unofficial issues in order to work on their official job responsibilities).

If this is the case, you may want to take your colleague out for a casual conversation. Be thoughtful in your discussion and be certain to recognize the strengths he has with his people skills. Ask how he feels about being inundated with your team's personal problems. Follow up with a question about how this affects his productivity. To further the conversation and to support your point, reiterate how a decrease in his official performance can negatively impact the rest of the team and their work, especially if several people rely

Attitudinal Outrage

on his performance and his product in order to effectively work on their tasks.

He will more than likely relate to how his actions affect his team's productivity. He may also request ideas on how to kindly tell others "no" when they seek his personal opinion or skilled guidance. Together, brainstorm ways to handle the situation and keep everyone happy.

> *"Kind words can be short and easy to speak, but their echoes are truly endless."* ~ Mother Theresa

Chapter Four:
Lagging Leadership

Good teams rely on great leadership. When you think of winning teams and outstanding projects, it is difficult to imagine their success without great leadership. Your survey responses reveal an unfortunate trend: not all managers are great leaders. In fact, it appears that some managers have little leadership skill at all! I can see how these situations and lagging leadership can be tremendous pet peeves, as well as morale busters.

In my workshops, we often talk of the issue behind poor leadership. It appears that many of the mangers who lack leadership ability were actually tremendous employees, engineers, or professionals in general. From this excellence with their job, they are promoted to a managerial level, with little or no leadership training. This is where the trouble begins.

Not only is this person struggling with the new identity as manager, but he can also be lacking in the personal-skills needed to be a good leader. Through experience, newly appointed managers will probably learn these skills. Unfortunately, those who are on his first team may bear the brunt of his leadership ignorance.

Not all individuals have this problem within the management position, and not all individuals learn the soft-skills needed for high performance teams. The people-problems in this chapter relate to those who have not yet learned the value of people-skills or who have forgotten what it was like to be a hard-working front-line employee.

> *"Leadership is all about people. It is not about organizations. It is not about plans. It is not about strategies. It is all about people-- motivating people to get the job done. You have to be people-centered."*
> *~ Colin Powell*

Clueless

I have a supervisor who is literally clueless. On a regular basis, he needs to be reminded of my tasks and how they relate to our project deliverables. This would not bother me if I only had to remind him once, but more often than that is ridiculous. It's also important to know that my tasks weren't the only ones that were in question.

There could be a number of reasons for this manager's forgetful nature. Perhaps he is not forgetful at all. Perhaps he is attempting to check up on the project status using the back-door approach of reminders and reiteration. Sometimes this works well when dealing with a social loafer on a team, but dealing with the entire team in this manner may not be effective. If this is the case, be open with him and explain how this makes you feel.

It could be that your manager is new to the position and was accustomed to managing his own progress and process. Now that he has a team to lead, he simply may be trying to dot his i's and cross his t's. If this is the case, he may not be aware of his behavior, much less aware that these reminders decrease the trust in his leadership. In order to train your manager to remember who does what and why, you may want to casually ask him how he stays organized. Share ideas, as if you are interested in the process. Then pursue the questions that relate to how he felt or would feel if his manager forgot his duties and he constantly had to remind him. Using the back door may give you insight, as well as a chance to condition him to stop this behavior.

A third possible reason behind the behavior may be that he is naturally impulsive, innovative, and (yes) disorganized in nature. Knowing this, a team meeting may be necessary to come up with a better system to recognize who is handling what task and how it relates to the big picture. Granted, this is not your job, but if you and your team are willing to sit with him for a few moments and get this organized, you may save precious time and prevent further frustration in the near future.

No matter what the reason behind the behavior, this scenario emphasizes the importance of a clear charter and flow chart. In this, each team member (including the leader) should have a copy of these documents. Granted, certain tasks change among altered parameters, but the big picture and overall understanding is important to have in order to decrease frustrations like this.

Wishy-Washy Leadership

You ask for pet peeves... my pet peeve is with managers who are indecisive or have a "do as I say, not as I do" attitude. How can we turn to these people for support or to assist with necessary change when they are wishy-washy or hypocritical?

I wonder how long individuals like this stay in their current position. I must agree that these aspects are two of my greater pet peeves as well. To me, this relates to the game of politics: Say one thing, do another, get appointed and increase power. The issue then becomes: what do these people do with this power and how many people did they step on to get there?

Most of the time, people in this position are not making the decisions themselves. They are answering to a higher authority. This makes the manager look indecisive and hypocritical. In reality, they work the system for promotion, to become the higher power that makes the decisions and pulls the strings.

Depending on the relationship with your manager, it may benefit all involved if you have an assertive, honest and diplomatic discussion. In this, address the lack of trust or respect that may permeate the team because of the indecisive or hypocritical behavior. If he is interested in the team's performance, this may be the first step to greater awareness and lesser indecisiveness. If he is not interested in the team's performance, he will shrug off your observations, say one thing and do another.

> *"A hypocrite is the kind of politician who would cut down a redwood tree, then mount the stump and make a speech for conservation."*
> ~ Adlai E. Stevenson

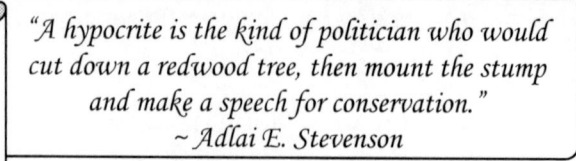

State of Confusion

I had a horrible manager (who is no longer in a management position) and one of my issues with him dealt with his autocratic decisions. Now, I understand autocratic decisions are made by managers, and I am fine with that responsibility. However, this supervisor would make a decision and after we finally adjusted to it and put our smiles back on, he would make a new decision that contradicted the first and we had to start over, in a terrible state of confusion! Mind you, this contradiction occurred numerous times and we basically gave up on his abilities.

Apparently, he got what was coming to him. One of the important abilities of strong managers and good leaders is the ability to make decisions, no matter how unpopular. The other important piece is the ability to stand by that decision. Furthermore, if a manager is not certain which option to choose, it is fine (and probably preferred) that they put off making a decision until research and fact is in play, if time permits. However, consider how much time and resources are wasted when a decision is made in haste and then changed, not once, but multiple times. This is not even good crisis management. Actions like this are impulsive and detrimental to the resources of the project.

When this decision-making process is the norm for an organization, it may be that the organization will not last long because of wasted resources and time. With all that said, I am not sure of the complexities behind this. Perhaps your supervisor was acting from misinformation from outside parties, or from request from upper management. Whatever the case, it is important that we don't misjudge the situation.

The best way to understand why people behave the way they do, or make the decisions they do, is to simply ask them. In this, you may take the back door approach and ask whether or not there is a time-line for the decision. If the time line is not critical, then ask how your team can help research or brainstorm cost-effective and time-sensitive options.

Managers who are focused on both the results and the team will take this opportunity to gather your input. Managers who are focused on the next step or who have no control will lose the team's respect and the opportunity for great leadership.

Pretend Democracy

My supervisor had a tendency to make decisions without consulting employees, then she made it sound like the employees had made the decision and were all for it (and usually, we did not like the decision and were against it).

It sounds as if collaborative decision making is a façade in your department. This type of behavior ranks right up there with stealing someone's idea and taking all the credit, except this time, your team also takes the fall if her decision was a poor one.

Not knowing the magnitude of these decisions or whom they affect, it is difficult to say why this type of behavior occurs. It could be that she is truly trying to save her own skin by laying the costs of the decision at your feet. When people do this, it is because they know a group may be able to better handle the fall out than a single individual. The only problem with this is that the manager is secluding herself from the team, and this speaks volumes.

How do you handle this situation? If you recall, I noted people are conditioned. We are trained. We follow particular patterns of behavior that have been proven or that are comfortable for us. This same concept applies herein. For instance, if you continue to ignore this behavior, more than likely, this behavior will continue. It seems like an endless cycle. However, if you address this as unacceptable behavior from a supervisor, then it may at least be curbed.

I understand it is not easy to address a manager's undesirable behavior, but it is possible to coach and communicate on all levels. What makes this coaching and communication critical is the fact that she used your group to make unpopular and undesired decisions. By including you in the picture, she has opened the door for an assertive conversation or a coaching approach.

> *"Change from the top down happens at the will and whim of those below."* ~ Peter Block

Inhumane at Work

One of my greatest pet peeves is when bosses leave their social skills at home. They don't seem to know how to be humane at work. Often, this also means they are quick to judge who you are based on a few characteristics or physical traits.

There seems to be a number of issues going on with these bosses. Some managers may be less skilled in the personal aspects of work. This can be addressed with training, but only if those bosses perceive this as an issue and if they desire to improve their leadership abilities. Research shows that individuals who are not humane at work generally do not succeed. The downfall to this is that demotion does not happen overnight and individuals in the early teams tend to suffer.

When working with a boss of this nature, it is probable that she is quite considerate of the project and seeks solid results. You can emphasize these aspects when meeting with her about her interactions with you or your team members. If she understands that her uncaring attitude can negatively affect productivity, she may be very willing to improve her ways so that you can improve yours.

If she continues to show a lack of respect or humanity in the workplace and it obviously hampers performance, her supervisor may be well aware of the dilemma. If not, and you have already tried the appropriate channels with little success, it may be that additional communication is necessary with higher channels. This is something you would want to discuss with HR or other objective parties before taking critical action.

The second aspect of quickly judging an individual based on a few traits is something many of us do. One theory associated with this is the attribution theory, in which we make judgment calls based on various attributions. Many times, this leads to an error in judgment, called the Fundamental Attribution Error.

    I have made this error many times, and now I practice to be aware of various possibilities for a person's behavior. If I can offer them the benefit of the doubt, I at least respond in a more positive tone, and this can lead to greater opportunities or more accurate understanding. While we can't force others to not make this error, we can control our reactions and our attributions.

    If this individual continues to error in judgment, it may call for an informal discussion where you can casually address these issues. If this does not work, then a more direct conversation may be appropriate. If these actions are serious and destructive, and after multiple attempts to decrease the behavior, it could be grounds for legal proceedings. At this stage, I would suggest you take this up with your attorney and the HR department.

> *"Good judgment comes from experience, and often experience comes from bad judgment."* ~
> Rita Mae Brown

Car 54: Where are You?

Car 54, where are you? -- This says it all. I can't stand it when managers aren't available, or can't be located, especially when we are at a crucial pass in the project.

This problem is not limited to those in managerial positions. Coffee breaks, smoke breaks, meetings, and other incidents may make it difficult to connect with individuals. This can be very frustrating when we can not find someone and we need an answer almost immediately.

Unfortunately, most people do not have ESP, but if a project is at a critical juncture, you would think the managers would be accessible. This is not always the case. If this is an isolated incident, then it may have simply been poor timing. If the inaccessibility is a frequent occurrence, it may be that your manager either has an uncanny case of subconscious avoidance, or she is encouraging your autonomy and group cohesion.

If this is a pattern, you may want to voice your concern over the lack of leadership presence. You may discover that your company forces your manager to constantly travel, leaving your team to gain a greater sense of independence and self-directed management skills. You may not be able to change this situation, but you can change the way you react to it. Your supervisor may also recognize this issue and, through brainstorming and collaboration, may agree to increase communication availability.

Flexible: To Be or Not To Be

My current corporate culture emphasizes that each work task must be tied to some process framework. My manager upholds this philosophy, even though the team seems to have lost some level of morale with this new guideline. We have different ways of working; many of us often stay way past "clock out" time, and take few breaks. Management does not seem to fret with this bend in the guidelines. However, my boss insists on penalizing us for coming in 5 minutes late (no meetings scheduled), even when we stayed 30 minutes later the night before or cut our lunch break in half. This seems trivial and she does not have the respect of her team. As long as our results meet the goals and we spend our allotted time at the lab, I don't understand why we spend extra time standardizing every facet of our jobs.

I believe this is one of the most universal complaints of a company. I can see the issue from both sides. On the one hand, I have met with organizations where

Lagging Leadership

the flexibility was abused. In a large organization, this can cost millions of dollars in mis-spent time and resources. Also, keep in mind that others on your team may be waiting for you to arrive so they can discuss a product or issue with you. When people are late, it may be a tremendous let down for team members.

On the other hand, I have seen companies lose valuable employees because of their double edged sword: they don't allow flexibility with timelines, but will not hesitate to keep employees late. The discontent with employees usually occurs when managers or guidelines penalize employees for arriving a few minutes late, but look the other way when employees stay late or have short lunches because of the nature of their work. This also costs the company valuable dollars, time and resources, as it is now necessary to fill those positions and evaluate why attrition may be high.

Much of this relates to the issue of motivation. There is much more at play than the simple problem of flexibility. Generally, the lack of flexibility is "the straw that broke the camel's back". There may be a lack of respect, of security, or of confidence permeating through veins of the company. They may have had a number of people abuse past flexibility, and this cost time and money. Your manager may simply have a tremendous drive for control.

Because of this, it may be very difficult to support any type of autonomy.

In general, if your company is not flexible but forces individuals to stay late or come in on days off, this is definitely a morale-buster and actually decreases productivity rather than increases performance. So how do you address this? First, discover whether this is a company policy or a managerial decision. If it is a company policy, then the decision to be made may be a personal one: should I stay or should I go? Once you make this decision, realize that your attitude and reactions are under your control. Both your attitude and your reactions can make your situation either better or worse: it is up to you.

If this is a managerial style, then it may be time to bring out the numbers. In a logical manner, reveal how this lack of flexibility impedes performance, which also negatively impacts her managerial results. You can cite research, or conduct research yourself (depending on how much time you have or how important it is to change the situation). The research you can conduct includes tracking how many times your team comes in late, versus how many times they stay late or don't take the required breaks. If your team is respectful of time, you may discover that you spend much more time at work and these facts may spur some flexibility. You can conduct this research as a team, or suggest your manager facilitate this study. Either way, someone's eyes may be opened: either yours because team members may be abusing time and resources, or your managers because team members are spending many more hours on-the-job than they are slacking off.

Stubborn or Inflexible

One manager wanted to cut cell phone costs. I presented several options with pros, cons, and risks to him. He was not interested in the potential obstacles or in the details of the hazards. In fact, he seemed confused by any of these options and explanations. He just wanted to know the quickest way to get the ball rolling. He didn't care about other manager's reservations either. As a result, his decision actually led to rising cell phone costs, and these costs rolled over him!

Is this a case of being stubborn or was there more to this story? It is hard to tell. In an issue like this, I wonder if there was a deadline regarding the decision and this manager waited until the last minute to decide. Either way, it appears that he is at fault for not listening to all of the research you provided or for not allowing ample time to review the information and make an informed, objective decision.

This scenario can be disconcerting, as we all hope our managers and upper level personnel have the skill or wherewithal to weigh options and choose the best for the allocated resources. Being that this did not seem like a crisis management decision, it would be an optimal situation to review all possibilities and make a solid choice.

Since you researched the options and presented them to your manager, I do not know if there was much else you could have done. I hope this was a learning experience for all involved, and that your manager's judgment has improved from the experience.

> *"What you always do before you make a decision is consult. The best public policy is made when you are listening to people who are going to be impacted. Then, once policy is determined, you call on them to help you sell it."* ~ Elizabeth Dole

Divide and Conquer

I had a manager who literally lied to us about things in the corporate world. He would tell different stories to different people *about the same subject. Not only was this deceptive, but it destroyed any possibility of team cohesion and team productivity. His motto appeared to be, "divide and conquer."*

This is a common behavior with teenaged girls: telling one story to one friend and a different story to a different friend. Funny enough, she always has an agenda for this story-telling behavior.

Obviously, these actions aren't limited to teenaged girls. My question is: why would your manager engage in this behavior? What is the reason for these different stories? The only way to handle the conflict that spurs between teenaged girls is to get them all together and get the stories out in the open. It is the only way you can clear the air. The same may be true of this situation.

In order to prevent further rumors or conflict, a meeting with everyone involved is in order. Gather your team and head to the conference room. Be certain everyone understands what will be discussed, so no one will feel defensive or surprised. It is important to not lay blame, but to unveil the truth and put the puzzle pieces together so you can see the big picture.

In this meeting, you may discover that your manager has told different versions of the story because he feels certain pieces were important only to certain people. He may be very unaware of the conflict or confusion caused by these actions. On the positive side, he may discover that your team can handle all sides of the story and that he does not have to shield anyone from any perspective. He may also realize that your team is interested in the greater picture, as well as the details important to each individual. The only way you can find out how he will react is to have the meeting and clarify the instances.

Under My Thumb

One of my previous bosses had a pure dictatorial way of leading, if you can even call it leading. His actions seemed to prompt a tremendous lack of self esteem in my department. He apparently had no technical skills. This was not because he had tremendous people skills, because his level of social skills was even worse than his technical skills. He appeared to be squelching everyone under him when he was craving promotion.

People in this position rarely succeed in the long run. Many outstanding leaders and leadership trainers will tell you that social skills are just as important as job skills. You can't get far with one and not the other. Ultimately, an imbalance like this is a glass ceiling, making it nearly impossible for individuals to advance to a higher professional position.

How you approach this individual depends on his focus and drive. If you feel he is focused on the project and is driven towards results, reiterate that when you talk to him about his communication (or lack thereof). Work the conversation so he thinks he is in control. Ask open ended questions and speaking in terms of logic and results. Be certain not to inundate the discussion with emotions or feeling words, as he will probably tune out of the conversation and waste your time.

Ask how your team can help him with his goals for advancement. Emphasize the importance of motivating team members and enhancing morale. From here, you can logically take the conversation to your team's need for rewards, empowerment, and communication. Bring about your greatest concerns and be specific as to how these concerns negatively impact performance.

Furthermore, it is important that you provide possible solutions and that you work with him to improve the situation. This could include a collaborative discussion that explores a number of scenarios and solutions that will improve his advancement, as well as morale and motivation for your team.

Remember, he is all about his professional advancement. If you scratch his back, he'll scratch yours. Focus on the results and how he can benefit, and your discussion should prove valuable and effective.

If none of this works, it may be time to consider your options and to discuss those options with appropriate channels.

> *"The key to successful leadership today is influence, not authority."* ~ Kenneth Blanchard

Chapter Five:

(De-) Motivational Mind-games

Anyone can tell you: motivation is a critical element for productivity and performance. When people are not motivated, performance drops. When performance drops, productivity drops. When productivity drops, customers and management voice their displeasure. When this occurs, people anxiously evaluate why productivity has dropped. If they do not attend to the motivational factors, any other solutions they attempt will more than likely fail. It is as if you are treating a wound. If you just see the wound and bandage it, it probably will not stop the bleeding. In order to stop the bleeding, physicians evaluate the wound, treat it, stitch it, bandage it, and follow up to make certain it has healed. Skipping any of these steps may cause infection, or may lead to a slower healing process or no healing at all.

The same principle applies to motivation and productivity. Unfortunately, many who wind up in leadership positions do not understand the importance of motivation, or they do not understand how to motivate.

One of the greatest misnomers about motivation is that it has to be materialistic to work. This is not the case. In fact, intrinsic motivation, or motivation from joy or desire, tends to be stronger than extrinsic motivation, or motivation from materialistic rewards.

Some of the most powerful rewards connected to intrinsic motivation include joy, success, fun, belonging, empowerment, independence, and intellectual stimulation. If a manager wishes to lead a high performance team, he must incorporate these aspects into the workplace or the task.

As you might suspect, if the opposite is presented to a team, that team struggles to perform well. Morale sinks and productivity falls. This chapter addresses some of these de-motivational mind games and, in many instances, how to manage them.

Finding a Scapegoat

I had a manager who was in the process of taking over support of an application from the vendor who produced it. She always tried to find a scapegoat on our team to blame if the transition of support was unsuccessful. She should have focused her time on how to make the transition successful. Her actions bred apprehension and fear in the team during this transitional process.

This is a classic example of how a lack in motivational elements will lead to disconcertment and a lack of productivity. Many would note this as the "self-fulfilling prophecy" in that your manager is looking for a way to fail and a person to blame for that failure.

People tend to focus on either success or failure. When we focus on success, we are programmed to find ways to make that situation successful. We seek solutions that fit into our scheme of success. The same holds true for failure. When we focus on failure, we are programmed to find ways that lead to a failing situation. We seek reasons that fit into our scheme of potential failure.

You are astute in recognizing that reframing her focus from failure to success could actually have enhanced team productivity and performance. This could lead to a successful transition. While she may feel the need to plan for failure, you can also bring to her attention the need to plan for success. For instance, ask how other transitions were successful. Discuss what is necessary to make the transition successful. Outline how she can heighten the productivity and morale of the team through the support's transition. By taking initiative to focus on the solutions and the successes, her perspective may change to recognize that your team can make this happen without issue.

> *"Mishaps are like knives, that either serve us or cut us, as we grasp them by the blade or the handle." ~ James Russell Lowell*

Negative Nelly

One of my biggest pet peeves is when managers only offer negative feedback, with little attention paid to successes.

This manager appears to have flunked Feedback 101. While there may not be much you can do to change the way managers offer feedback, you can remember this when you provide feedback to others.

Feedback is an important facet of performance. When people hear only negative feedback, they lose confidence and esteem. This decreases momentum and motivation within the task, and this can cost a company time and money.

When providing feedback, make certain to include the positive aspects of performance. When correcting an issue, refrain from excessive use of "you" in the topics. Instead, focus the corrective feedback on the project, not on the person. For instance, compare the following two options:

... Your presentation was not as thorough as we would have liked. You did not touch on the details of the budget, nor did you emphasize the project milestones. You need to address these issues before the next program meeting...

or:

... Yesterday's presentation was not as thorough as we would have liked. It did not touch on the details of the budget, nor did it emphasize the project milestones. How can these issues be addressed before the next program meeting?...

The word "you" is presented frequently in the first option. This term usually brings up defenses, and this means the person addressed does not attend to the message but attends to defending his choices. Typically, this ruffles feathers and burns bridges more than it encourages greater performance and productivity.

The second option focuses on the project. It closes with a question, draws the listener in and gives him the attention and time he needs to process the issue and come up with a solution. This is a method of empowerment and a way to develop greater success and esteem. The message is the same: we had a problem, now you have to fix it. However, the delivery of the message is very different and will bring about different attitudes and productivity.

When you work with a manager who only offers negative feedback, try to reframe his message into one that is positive for you. Most of the time, the manager is focusing on how to make the project better, even if this means focusing on correcting problems. If you can mentally rephrase the feedback so the project, not you, is the subject of correction, then you may not take the feedback personally.

If your manager is new to management and appears eager to learn and develop leadership strengths, then coaching her through the importance of proper feedback can be quite valuable. In this, you may discuss the different responses people have to the each method of feedback. Once a manager sees the benefits of focusing on the task and the project, the delivery may change for the better.

The Screw Up

On a team of 12, there is one person that everyone on the project team has complained about. She frequently missed deadlines and basically was not performing in her assigned capacity. After multiple escalations to three levels of management over a 10 month period, she was finally reassigned. However, because management failed to act sooner, it caused a four-month delay on the project.

This is an unfortunate incident. It seems to occur all too often! The fact that management did take action is positive, even though its seemingly tardy response has delayed the project. In cases like these, there may be a number of reasons why change takes time to occur. For instance, there could have been a number of legal issues requiring extensive documentation and complaints from multiple levels. Whatever the case, changes were made.

Now, you have to manage the delay of the project and the frustration of the team caused by your saboteur. By revisiting your charter and clearly outlining your roles and responsibilities, you may be able to make up for lost time.

Micro-Management Nightmare

My supervisor was a micro-manager. She never let anyone work without severe instruction or constant supervision. This obviously hampered our creativity. Needless to say, morale was very low in our office.

Most people are very creative and need an outlet for that creativity. People also need to experience autonomy. Both are components of motivation. Without either, people feel stifled and stagnant. This occurs with micro-management. Any leadership training will teach you: leave the micromanagement technique at home. Forget it. Micromanagement does not work in the long run.

Please understand that there are some instances when micro-management is necessary, but to use this as a constant managerial method kills the very progress we desire.

Dealing with micro-managers can be tricky because the situation may be complex. Generally, micro-managers have a great need for control. This need for control must be addressed in conversation in order to get your point across.

For instance, schedule a brief meeting between you, a co-worker and your manager. Address the pitfalls your group experiences because of the micromanagement, and how this impedes results. Use logic and quantitative reasons that encourage your manager to release the reigns, if even for a trial period. She may find that her team is very competent and able to get things done in a way that meets even her expectations.

With experience, most managers find they are so busy that micromanagement is simply not feasible. Perhaps your supervisor has not managed many teams prior to yours. This lack of experience may be one element that supports her need to micromanage.

Management styles can be learned, depending on her previous team's performance. If this is the case, ask her what she expects of your team. Brainstorm solutions that meet her expectations as well as offer your members more autonomy. While she still remains in control, she does not have to be overly controlling.

> *"You never achieve real success unless you like what you are doing."* ~ Dale Carnegie

Busy Work

My boss had a tendency to give us last minute work requests. He assigns us work that isn't needed. It seems we work in order to make him look good, even if the tasks don't suit the project or align with the objectives.

Busy work... no one likes it. The concept of busy work probably stems all the way back to grade school, where students worked just to work. In the workplace, it seems like a misplacement of time and money.

Granted, sometimes the work assigned seems like busy work, but it truly is needed. We may not understand the importance of monthly reports or weekly informational meetings, but they may be crucial to others on the team or to various stakeholders.

If it will decrease the frustration, simply ask your manager about the importance of these reports. His response can either help you see the greater picture, or will reveal his lagging leadership and love for busywork.

If this work is hindering your project and if other managers are upset at this hindrance, then it may be necessary to speak to your manager about the issue. If his goal is to look good, then discuss how these tasks actually take away from his success.

If these assignments are necessary, then remember the overall picture when you prefer to work on other assignments. While these may not be enjoyable, they may be necessary to the overall success of the team and project.

Chapter Six:
Communication Corruption

So many problems in life can be traced back to poor communication. As you've seen through this book, if communication is not clear, big problems can arise.

Communication is also important when it comes to correcting these issues. Many of the suggestions in this book rely on communication. If you choose not to communicate the concerns or address the issues, then you choose to live with the problem person or pet peeve. For every choice, there is a consequence. Many of these choices and consequences have a solid foundation in communication (or lack thereof).

This chapter poses problems presented by individuals who experienced poor communication in the workplace. You can imagine how this poor communication negatively affects morale, productivity, and results. The opposite is also true: good communication positively affects morale, productivity, and results.

When you read through the next couple of chapters, pay attention to the issues at hand. Often times, we aren't aware of our own behaviors. This makes it difficult to recognize when our behaviors are undesirable. Until we recognize our own communication mishaps or pet peeve actions, we can't correct them. So, while reading through this book, ponder each of these issues and how they may relate to your actions and behaviors.

She Never Told Me

How can someone complete a task when they don't know the task was assigned to him? I ask this because it has happened to me. My co-worker committed me to timelines and deliverables without telling me. She never told me.

This appears to be a classic example of a lack of communication. She committed you to a project and never told you. So, who is to blame when the project goes bust?

If this is not an isolated incident with her, I would say she needs a better method of follow-up and you need to be assertive when you remind her that you were never informed of the new task. Instead of placing blame and finding fault, work to prevent this issue from occurring again. Collaborate ways to keep one another informed, especially when a decision may involve you.

If no one addresses the lack of communication, this behavior will contiue. Your manager may not be aware of the detriment caused by her actions. If she is not informed of this, you can't expect her to change, which means your situation won't change either.

Ramblin' Man

A couple of my employees tend to ramble and beat around the bush when I need a direct answer. This leads me to believe they do not know what is going on and I question their ability.

Instances like this can lead to great misunderstanding. Some people naturally prefer lengthier conversations that involve personal reflection and interaction. What they consider to be polite conversation, others consider to be beating around the bush. It is a simple difference in communication style, but if people aren't aware of this difference it can lead to tremendous misunderstanding and conflict.

One of the best ways to remedy this misunderstanding is to study various communication preferences. If this is not available to you, then try to reframe the situation.

For instance, step into their shoes and try to recognize their perspective. They may see you as harsh and uninterested. You may see them as gossipers and indirect. Both perspectives are correct, and both are incorrect.

When you visit with these employees, listen to their word choices. If they use feeling words, talk about their personal lives and invite others to join in the conversation, they may need to belong.

You may be quite the opposite, and this difference can create conflict. Ask your employees what motivates them. Ask them what they like to talk about. All of these things will give you insight to their behavior and communication style.

Obviously, this communication style is not appropriate all of the time. In this, speak with your employees about the need to be brief and to be succinct in their explanations. If you approach this diplomatically, these employees may see your point and will hopefully adjust their communication style.

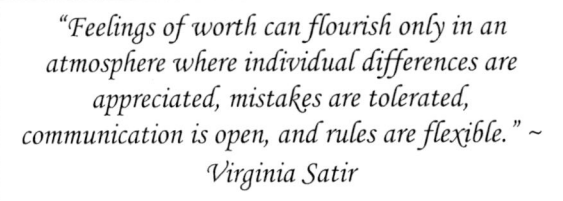

> *"Feelings of worth can flourish only in an atmosphere where individual differences are appreciated, mistakes are tolerated, communication is open, and rules are flexible."* ~ Virginia Satir

Nosy Nancy

I have a co-worker who always sticks her nose into conversations about issues (work-related) that do not concern her. Often, I'll stop by a cubicle to ask one person a specific question, only to have this other person answer the question.

Whether it is the nosy neighbor across the street or the interested individual in the next cubicle, many people want to know what is going on. Obviously, this can be very frustrating.

There are many ways to handle these actions. One of the worst things you can do is aggressively attack their behavior. This will only lead to bad feelings and tremendous conflict. One of the best things you can do is diplomatically talk to this person and voice your concern. Inform her that you respect her private conversations and hope she respects your conversations as well. Recognize that she strives for a sense of belonging, and that her actions actually distance her from the rest of the team. Ask her what solutions she may have for this issue and how you both can improve these relations.

After this diplomatic conversation, if her behavior does not change, then it may be time for assertive action. Remind her of your agreement and solution-focused discussion, and document some of the issues and poor feelings that are harbored because of her nosiness. Further, ask her to respect your privacy and conversations as much as you respect hers.

When you address this individual, it is important that you do so in terms of feelings, team, respect, and solutions. These are terms to which she may quickly relate.

What Do I Need to Know

I can't stand it when people don't completely answer my questions. They seem to withhold important information because they are territorial. For instance, I asked someone about a system and he provided only what I asked for. I found out there was much more I needed to know, and he knew it. If I knew that I needed to know that additional information, I would have asked, but what frustrated me was the fact that he knew I needed that information and he did not provide it to me.

When we study why information is purposefully withheld, it is often because the person withholding the information is protecting something. He could be protecting his chance for advancement or his need to be in control throughout the process.

Whatever the reason, it is proven that withholding information (knowingly or not), frequently leads to conflict, ill-will, misunderstandings, and team disruption. All of these lead to poor performance, wasted time, and exhausted resources.

If this person is truly hiding information in order to procure a new position, it will be very difficult to change this behavior. If this person kept this information from you because he wanted to be in control throughout the process, then you can brainstorm ways that will keep him in the loop as well as provide you with all of the information you need.

His actions are not healthy to a team or project. Eventually, he may be called on this behavior. I just hope your team is out of harm's way when this occurs.

Returned to Sender

One of my co-workers never seems to get the message, especially when it is delivered via email. It seems that if you want him to read anything, you have to print the email and physically stick it under his nose.

There are many people who simply breeze through emails. Some folks get over 100 emails every day! Some are too long; others are much too brief for the importance.

There are many pros and cons to using email, but when we truly take a step back, do we know if the individual has thoroughly read the information and understood what we were trying to say? It is difficult to say because the physical signs of body language or voice inflection are missing.

The only reason people read email is because they think it is important to them. What would make this email important to this person? If he thinks you are simply going to print the information and bring it to his attention anyway, he may think: "why bother reading the email if I'll get a printed version at the meeting?"

Perhaps he does not think the information is important to him, even though you do. In this case, mark it so he knows it is important to him, even if he does not think so at this point.

People also need to get into the habit of NOT sending emails to mass individuals. If a person tends to forward information to everyone on the list, when only a few need the information, the others will begin the habit of skimming the information or not reading the email at all! This is obviously not a habit we wish to cultivate in a technologically-advanced organization.

Emails can easily be forwarded to other individuals. They are also easily ignored. Both options have their advantages and disadvantages, but when you are seeking a solution to a problem and your email is shuffled around with no response to you, it seems like a hopeless pattern. Again, the best way to manage this is to make your email important to the recipient and include a clear deadline for notification.

Keep emails brief. Use bullet points instead of paragraphs (it is easier to read and process this way). If a person has questions, this also opens opportunity for detailed communication between you and that individual.

Depending on your inbox, many people request electronic verification that you have opened the email. Others flag the messages. Again, this won't mean anything if you flag every email or request verification for the messages that aren't important. It is important to assure these methods are still valuable.

Just like with any other communication, abusing the email system lowers its perceived level of importance or value. I know a gentleman who does not say much. He is a thinker and a listener. When he does say something, everyone listens

Communication Corruption

because they know it is important. This was learned through experience, just like experience conditions our perceptions and reactions to others.

> *"Every improvement in communication makes the bore more terrible."* ~ Frank Moore Colby

Timid Torments

We have a client whose timidity with her supervisors is impacting the contractors' work accomplishments.

Many people tend to passively behave when their job is at risk (and when it is not?). This does not mean to say that she may not complain to others about her supervisors, but she does not address these issues herself. The same can be said of any of these pet peeves or problem people.

Often, people would rather not address the problem itself out of fear of being considered a nag or a negative person. Instead, they gather in gaggles and complain about the same issue. This costs valuable time and money and is truly a waste of effort.

As I have mentioned before, this book offers suggestions to deal with these issues, but it may require that you step out of your comfort zone and actually communicate the problem and brainstorm the solution with those problem people. If all you do is complain about the issue, then nothing productive will be accomplished. If only one person continues to address these issues after the team complains, that person may be mislabeled, even if the team is very grateful for the action. This lack of support is not good for anyone and may tear a team apart. Don't rely on one person to speak for you. The burden may be heavy. Everyone needs to step up and be proactive.

The same goes for this client. She may fear conflict, or fear possible repercussions from her supervisors. However, if she were able to reframe the situation and see how this lack of action negatively impacts the work of contractors, she may be willing to make a few changes.

Someone like this probably enjoys the company of others, so use this opportunity to focus on solutions and win-win scenarios for all involved. This takes effort from both parties, so ask yourself: how important is this change?

Master Manipulator

There is one guy in our department who seems to be a master manipulator for conversation time. He has an extremely strong personality. He doesn't listen to others and he has pre-conceived notions to issues not yet presented. When the discussion is not going the way he thinks it should, he is very domineering and takes control of the conversation (even if he is not lead of the meeting). He seems to be overly ambitious and competitive. Email has been the most effective way for me to communicate with this individual.

These actions may be related to a particular personality style. They may be related to ambition to for promotion. No matter what the reason, it is important to match his communication to get your point across.

If he speaks quickly, then match it. If he uses specific terms (i.e. logic instead of intuition, big picture instead of detail), then use those same terms. Most of the time, these people enjoy being in control of the conversation. Ask open ended questions that lead him to believe he is control, while you steer him in the direction you want the conversation to go.

If you facilitate the meeting, you can use your body language or voice inflections to interrupt him (yes, you can interrupt) and move onto the next topic on your agenda. Use phrases like, "Aha... Bill, that is an excellent point for another day. Let's table that and discuss it later" or "That is an interesting thought, Leigh, let's see what others think about it..." These types of polite interruptions may easily move you to your next item on the list, while not ruffling any feathers.

If this employee's domineering behavior escalates and deters productivity, it may be time for your supervisor to step in. Unless your boss is in a fog, he may have seen these same behaviors and is aware of the need for intervention.

Keep in mind we can't change others, but we can change our responses to others. In that, your recognition that email is an effective form of communication is a great recognition. If nothing else changes, you can continue to rely on this to get your message across without interruption or domination.

> *"You can have power over people as long as you don't take everything away from them. But when you've robbed a man of everything, he's no longer in your power."* ~ Aleksandr I. Solzhenitsyn

Chapter Seven:
Poor Presentation

This chapter is an interesting one because it covers topics like professionalism and meeting etiquette. Many of your pet peeves were universal and this made the chapter easy to organize and write.

Studies show that the environment is an important piece of performance and productivity. You can find a seemingly endless amount of research that outlines the necessary elements for a highly productive environment. What we are going to discuss in this chapter are environmental no-no's. Many of these pet peeves are people-problems.

When people don't realize that their behaviors annoy or disrespect others, they don't realize it is time to stop those behaviors. What I highly recommend you do

Poor Presentation

with this chapter is carefully read each pet peeve and objectively consider whether or not you are also guilty of these behaviors. If you find yourself practicing some of these pet-peeve actions while you are at work, it may be time to change your behavior for the benefit of everyone around you.

If you find some of these pet peeves in your office, there is a way to address this. Send out an anonymous survey to your team. In this survey, ask them what their pet peeves are. They can anonymously submit these and share them in a meeting. From here, no names are mentioned and it is kept as objective as possible. With these surveys, you can take it further and ask your team how you can prevent these issues from hurting your department (as if your team doesn't have these pet peeves, even if your team does!) It could be considered to be a team-building experience, especially if you keep it in a positive mindset and keep it objective and without blame.

Missing Meeting Etiquette

My biggest pet peeve has to do with meeting etiquette. Most people don't seem to have any! For goodness sake, start and end the meetings on time and send an agenda. Make sure to follow that agenda, or why bother sending it?

Meeting etiquette appears to be a lost art and because of this, meetings last at least 1/3 longer than they should. Once individuals experience organized and productive meetings, they become very accustomed to this type of structure. This decreases the amount of time and money wasted in non-productive meetings.

I agree with the thought that each meeting should have an agenda and the agenda should be followed. Trainers who facilitate programs in meeting management will spend hours training people how to write an agenda and how to follow it. This is an important piece of effective meeting management and many actually consider it to be the necessary cornerstone. If you find that your meetings are inefficient or ineffective, it could be that the agenda is not accurate or is not followed. Either way, most management and meeting leads would jump at a solution to decrease wasted time and increase productivity. Encourage an agenda and follow its structure.

When people have an agenda, the meeting does not have to be so structured that creativity is stifled. In fact, many meetings include time simply for creative banter regarding a particular issue. As long as the people in attendance recognize what will be discussed and when, they will be prepared for that discussion.

One other note listed in this pet peeve was timing. One major "don't" of meetings is to ignore the timeframe. This means beginning or ending late. This usually sends the message that the participants' time is not important, and this is construed as disrespectful.

Many wait for the last-minute attendees and this is why they begin late. These last-minute attendees know you will wait for them, so their behavior does not change. You wait for them, so your behavior does not change. This waste's everyone else's time. Whatever you do, don't reinforce undesirable behavior like showing up late to a meeting. Address it. Announce the expectations. Don't reinforce it.

Agenda Issues

I can't stand disorganized and rambling meetings. They seem to be a direct result of poor scheduling or conducting a meeting without a published agenda. A project manager should NEVER schedule or conduct a meeting without a published agenda.

This pet peeve reiterates the importance of the agenda. Because of this theme, here are some tips to a strong agenda and an efficient meeting:

1. Describe the objectives of the meeting. Don't have a meeting just to have a meeting. A meeting must have a purpose. In the agenda, note whether the meeting is scheduled to a.) make a decision, b.) inform of change or progress, c.) manage conflict or resolve issues, or d.) sell your idea to others
2. Outline the schedule and the time involved for each topic to be addressed, even if this means noting that a creative-thinking session will occur from 8-8:30.
3. Note the definition of roles. For instance: Johnny is the meeting lead, Henry is the recorder and Katrina is the timer to keep us on track. Each of these roles is important if you want an effective meeting. I would rotate the roles as much as possible, so no one person is "stuck" as lead, recorder, or timer.

And:

4. Note how follow-up will be conducted. A meeting may not mean anything if there is no follow-through.

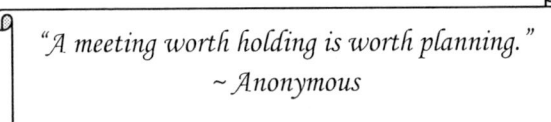

"A meeting worth holding is worth planning."
~ Anonymous

Due When?

I have an employee who continually drops off reports for review at the end of the due date. He leaves for the afternoon and any questions I may have for this report has to wait until I find him the next day.

This fellow may be a procrastinator. Since he has waited until the end of the day to hand in his report, he may be nervous regarding the feedback about the report. In this, many people like him drop things off at the last minute in order to avoid any harsh comments. Usually, they hope that whatever questions or comments you may have will "soften" as you wait to meet with them again. If you find this is habit and you do not address it, you allow it continue.

Some people recognize that turning a task in by the end of the due date is still turning it in on time. Factually, this is accurate. However, if you are not comfortable with this process, perhaps your behavior will be the easiest to change.

During one of my workshops, we discussed people who wait until the last minute to turn in their report. What many found to be an effective strategy was offering these individuals a "false deadline". If you know this individual will wait until the end of the deadline day to turn in his information, then you move up the deadline to noon, 9:00 am or the day prior.

Colorful Enthusiasm

There is a 29 year-old in our office who wears suits and ties to work to maximize his image (our office is more business casual, so his appearance stands out). He names his attire each day, "today I am wearing Lavender Haze, tomorrow maybe it'll be Burgundy Waterfall." His goal is to see how many executives he can meet in the hallway. He times his trips to the shredder so he can run into them.

It sounds like you have a go-getter on your hands. If this behavior does not hamper anyone's performance, it may be annoying but harmless. However, if the executives are annoyed with this behavior, someone needs to kindly mention to him that these actions could actually impede his advancement instead of promote it.

Explain that enthusiasm may be perceived as desperation. When this is the case, most people don't want to deal with desperate people. The truth is, whether desperate or overly enthusiastic, some behavior may be construed as annoying and no one wants to share space with an annoying person.

The Profane

One of the most unprofessional things people can do is use profanity in the office or insult clients while other customers are around. This happens in my office and it is very discouraging to those of us who try to be professional. It seems as if they don't respect anyone else.

As I mentioned in the beginning of this chapter, the concept of professionalism seems to be a lost art. Many of you wrote in about this very same problem and it does not seem to be going away.

One of the only ways to effectively handle this situation is to deal with it head on. Some people may be intimidated and do not want to address these abrasive folks about their bad habits. This can lead to office bullying, and this is definitely not healthy for the team or the company. To prevent this, it is important to get management on board.

If management behaves this way, then approach your manager about the unprofessional behavior within the office. Talk about how a customer may have heard someone complaining about a different client and how this affects relations. Discuss vulgarities and how they do not match the team or organizational objectives.

Once your manager understands how these behaviors impede productivity, you can then focus on the fact that she is the one behind all of this!

If none of this works, a hostile environment such as this could be cause for a visit with HR.

> *"Profanity is the crutch of the conversational cripple."* ~ Jay Alexander

More Meeting Mistakes

When I lead a meeting, one individual constantly checks his email on his blackberry. Another individual's cell phone rings. A different person spends the entire meeting clicking his pen. All of these are distracting and are pet peeves of mine.

This brings us back to meeting etiquette. One of the best ways to attack the lack of meeting etiquette is to have a meeting (with an agenda) that outlines the expectations for each meeting you have. This includes specifying what behavior is and is not acceptable. This may be a brief, informational meeting. You can explain to your team that the lack of etiquette wastes everyone's time and can be perceived as disrespectful. Then mention how you respect everyone's time and hope these expectations will cut down on the amount of necessary meeting time.

Ask your team members to design the expectations and the consequences. When they are involved and design the guidelines, they are much more likely to adhere to the expectations. Most make the mistake of writing the rules and handing them out to everyone. While this can be effective some of the time, it is usually construed as controlling and is not well accepted. But when you work with your team and allow them to design the rules, then it is a team effort with little blame on any one person.

This not only works to design expectations for meeting etiquette, but it will also be effective to support company policy regarding personal interaction over the phone or internet. As long as you have a forum where your team members design the expectations and consequences, they may be more apt to understand and buy-in to those guidelines.

Footsies

I have a young tech staff member on my team. During meetings, he usually lays on the floor (this drives me nuts!) One day, I was giving instruction and he put his feet (no shoes, just socks) on my desk.

Take a moment to think about this issue. What would you do? Now, approach this from an issue where bridges can not be burned... how would you approach this? Most people who have reached the point of no return say they would slap those feet of their desk. I could see this, but it may not be the most effective first attempt.

One of the first things to do is to address your employee in private about his actions in the meeting. While you may encourage comfort in your meetings, there are boundaries which this gentleman has crossed. Keep in mind, if you have not worked with your team to design these boundaries, many may not know what they are and they will not know when they have crossed those lines.

When you speak with this employee, emphasize the fact that you encourage comfort, as long as it is within the context of professionalism. Ask him what he thinks he can do to be both comfortable and professional in a meeting. Someone like this may have some creative ways to incorporate both needs of comfort and professionalism.

And if this doesn't work, slap his feet off of your desk ☺.

Sweet or Sour

We have a young woman in our office who has a very sweet nature. However, she is perpetually late to meetings and to work. When she does finally show, she sweetly proposes her excuse and everyone lets it slide. In the background, everyone else complains. When I approached my manager about her behavior, my manager said, "...but she is so sweet." To me, this is inconsiderate behavior and shows a lack of respect for the rest of us. So, is she really that sweet?

Whether someone is too sweet to ignore or too hostile to handle, the behavior does need to be addressed. The unfortunate news is that even your boss has been sucked into the sugary vacuum.

Your co-worker may shy from conflict, which means whenever corrected, her defenses activate and she does not hear a word. With people like this, it is important to not focus on the person, but to focus on the problem itself. This may also be more effective if you ask this co-worker how this type of behavior can affect a team. Further that by asking her how this type of behavior can be prevented and what she or others may do to be more respectful of their co-worker's time and resources. Usually when someone sees how their actions can hurt team members, they are more likely to change behavior in order to support their team. When you address it as her issue relating to company policy, she may not see how it is a "big deal" and will sweetly make excuses.

Cubicle Annoyances

We work in a world of cubicles. It is difficult to work in this setting when people are not respectable of those around them. They use their phones on speaker, they speak loudly, and they pop gum or snort and sniff without use of Kleenex.

It sounds as if you've got some noisy neighbors. When I studied ergonomics and workplace environment, the issue of noise was one of the biggest deterrents to productivity. When people are deep in thought and interrupted by someone snorting and choking, it can offset the momentum.

Usually, many people are frustrated by this annoyance, but maybe only one team member will speak up. It is important that this one person is not seen as the scapegoat, since he has done the entire workplace a favor. He has stuck his neck out to address the annoyances of a co-worker that affect the entire department's productivity.

Poor Presentation

With this in mind, these annoyances won't stop until someone addresses them. Many people are simply unaware that their bad habits are affecting the work abilities of others. If this is a team decision, you may take a few minutes in a meeting to address personal annoyances. Like before, keep all names and identifying features out of conversation, but note any common annoyances that are preventable. You can even preface the meeting with, "I've recently read text noting that personal annoyances impede workplace performance. I want to be sure we all have a pleasant environment in which to work. Let's talk about some of the most common annoyances and brainstorm ways to prevent these from impeding our work."

After this meeting, if you still see the undesirable behaviors in your team, you can address each individual in private, again noting the solutions your team came up with in the meeting.

With this back door approach, you are not seen as the bad guy, but you help to clean up your department.

> *"It is the individual who is not interested in his fellow men who has the greatest difficulties in life and provides the greatest injury to others."* ~ *Alfred Adler*

Conclusion

People deal with pet peeves and problem people every day. The best way to handle these incidents is to first understand the behavior and then to respond to it in a way that is constructive, effective, and respectful.

The problems discussed herein were the most common presented to me through a nation-wide survey of project managers and professional office employees. I hope the responses offered some explanation as to why these actions may occur. Not only that, I hope this inspired possible win-win solutions from the examples provided.

As we've discussed throughout the book, not everyone realizes they are the source of the pet peeve. This may include you! As you read through this book, I also hope you were able to recognize some of the most common pet peeve behaviors and objectively evaluate whether or not you are a pet peeve source.

Conclusion

While we wish everyone recognized their annoying behavior and changed without expression from us, this is not usually the case. Remember that we can not change others, but we can change our reaction to others. In this, we can also change how we interact with others, which may spur others to change their own behavior. One critical element to all of this is communication.

Without communication, we don't recognize boundaries or frustrations, nor do we recognize the need to change. Nearly every one of the solutions discussed in this book involves communication with the problem person. This type of confrontation or coaching is learned and should be practiced. Keep the discussion objective, rational, kind and task-focused. Refrain from personalizing the issue.

My best of luck to you as you address these issues. By decreasing pet peeves and people problems in your workplace, you will likely save your team and organization precious time and resources. You will also save your team from unnecessary frustration and headache!

About Dr. Dawdy

Reach Peak Potential with Peak Strategies: An organizational training, executive coaching, leadership development firm.

Gwynne N. Dawdy is an Organizational Psychologist and a National Certified Counselor. She is an experienced consultant in the fields of leadership development, personality and social styles, team management, conflict resolution, communication, sport psychology, and health wellness.

She has a Ph.D. in industrial/organizational psychology; a MS specialized in sport psychology, and a MA in counseling and psychology. She is a trainer, consultant, executive coach and author.

Dr. Dawdy's professional experiences include training, coaching, and consulting in the fields of performance enhancement, accelerated project/team management skills, leadership, group cohesion, communication, relationships, goal getting, motivation, and stress management.

Training Topics and Services:

Interpersonal Relations
Social Styles and Behavioral Preferences
Communication Styles
Leadership Development
Coaching in the Workplace
Team Cohesion
Motivation
Conflict Resolution
Goal Achievement
Sport Psychology
Performance Enhancement

We specialize in ½ or full day workshops, teleseminars, and executive coaching for project managers, team leaders, and high potential personnel. These trainings are often conducted on-site or as open-enrollment courses for project management chapters, corporations, and other organizations. Many of our participants are leaders, project managers, human resource personnel, and educators who strive for greater success with less human effort.

Living and using one's talents and potential to the fullest is optimal in many areas of life. In order to do this, one must be able to recognize the mental pitfalls and prevent them from engulfing performance and thoughts.

Some of these mental pitfalls include:
Interpersonal relation issues

Ineffective communication
Motivational issues
Unclear goals
Low confidence
Fear of failure or of success
Stress or health issues

Dr. Dawdy's seminars and consultations are designed to troubleshoot these issues. Clients will learn to strengthen various aspects that effect work performance. This will help increase performance, confidence, management skills, and even physical and mental wellness and health. With these strategies, people can enhance their productivity and their personal connections.

Contact Peak Strategies for more information, or to view or purchase additional products or services:

http://peakstrategies.net
ps@peakstrategies.net

P.O. Box 7034
Woodland Park, CO 80863

Peak Strategies
Training Coaching Development

Index

Administrative (non-)Assistant	63
Agenda Issues	122
Bad Attitude Bob	58
Busy Work	102
Car 54: Where are You	82
Clueless	72
Colorful Enthusiasm	125
Complainers	26
Criticized	24
Cubicle Annoyances	131
Curbed Creativity	55
Divide and Conquer	87
Drama Queen	60

Index

Due When	124
Emotional Apathy	53
ESP Expectations	44
Fault Finder	18
Finding a Scapegoat	95
Flexible: To Be or Not To Be	83
Foggy Feedback	43
Footsies	128
He Doesn't Work	30
Helping or Hindering	69
I Wasn't Told	20
Inhumane at Work	79
Instant Promotion	56
It Can't Be Done	51
It's All About Me	67
Later Never Comes	42
Master Manipulator	115
Micro-management Nightmare	100

Missing Meeting Etiquette	120
More Meeting Mistakes	127
Negative Nelly	96
News via Gossip	37
Nosy Nancy	109
Playing the Victim	32
Preparing to Fail	64
Pretend Democracy	78
Profane (The)	126
Ramblin' Man	107
Resentful	66
Returned to Sender	111
Right on Track	40
Rumors	22
Screw-Up (The)	99
She Never Told Me	106
Social Loafers	61
State of Confusion	76

Index

Stubborn or Inflexible	86
Sweet or Sour	130
Timid Torments	114
Too Much Work	28
Tunnel Vision Boss	38
Under My Thumb	89
Undermining Saboteur	49
What Do I Need to Know	110
Wishy-Washy Leadership	74

Printed in the United States
74364LV00002B/1-99